Clarity
for Your Day

SHARAM

EDITED BY
Shahed & Nafiseh

TALIA

CLARITY FOR YOUR DAY
SHARAM

Edited by: Shahed & Nafiseh
Paperback 1st Edition
Published in 2020 by:

Talia, Friends of Existence, Inc.
Website: www.taliafriends.org
Email: talia@taliafriends.org

Copyright © 2020 by Talia, Friends of Existence, Inc.
ISBN 978-0-9600047-2-0

All rights reserved.

No part of this book may be reproduced, stored in a retrieval system, or transmitted in any form or by any means, electronic, mechanical, photocopying, recording or otherwise, without the prior written permission of the publisher.

Many thanks to Melina H, Stefan Hoelscher, and Chris Pearson for their invaluable help.
Cover Art & Paintings: Sharam
Page Layout & Book Design: No Mind Design

More Books
by Sharam

Order now on:
SharamLove.com

Don't Beat Yourself Up

You Are Your Happiness

The Book of Existence
Part One

Mysticism
The Psychology of Love

Happiness
The Essence of Your Being

Decoding Love
Understanding is Compassion

From Negativity to Joy

The Power of Let-Go

Happiness
The Name of Our Soul

INTRODUCTION

Our minds are complicated. They are based on the past and usually the negative past. The mind brings memories and emotions from our past and complicates the present. It makes it difflcult to see clearly what is happening right now. We color what is happening now with what we have experienced in the past through our minds. This complicated mind gets involved with our work, our relationships, and our ability to love. It gets involved with everything, making life confusing and unsatisfying. When our mind steps aside or becomes quiet, we become clear. Life becomes simple and we experience joy, connection, and contentment. In "Clarity for Your Day" we learn to recognize the mind and how it limits our freedom and our ability to love. Sharam shares how, with acceptance and awareness, we can move beyond the mind and operate from our soul. You can read the book cover-to-cover, or choose one at random for your day.

Calmness brings clarity and clarity brings understanding. Understanding is clarity of the mind. When we are calm, the mind slows down and we become clear. When you are clear, you have acceptance. Calmness of the mind comes from meditation, which leads to bliss. Understanding, love, acceptance, clarity, feeling the moment—all lead to bliss. When understanding comes, the ego subsides. When love comes, also the ego subsides. Anything that causes the ego to subside leads to bliss.

Love with the ego or the mind is lower love. It is always dual, which means: if love is there, hate is there also. Lower love is a conditional love. If someone does something we like or something that makes us feel good, we love them. If, on the other hand, they do something we don't like, we just don't like them. If they give us attention and make us feel important, again we love them. If not, we fall apart. If they don't love us, we feel valueless and hate ourselves. The lower love or this love/hate relationship is never satisfying. We might occasionally get a hint of the joy that higher love offers, but never enough to be truly satisfied. Love is good, but we have to go to the higher love.

To get to this higher love, we need a deep understanding of lower love. Too often on the path of love, we just want to be loved. But without really looking into ourselves and the nature of lower love, we can never be truly satisfied, never be truly enlightened, because hate is always just around the corner.

Understanding doesn't come through the mind; it comes from our soul. It comes when the mind steps aside. The only thing that puts our mind aside is love. When we feel pure love, we feel the ecstasy of our soul. Every time we feel love, it helps our growth. When we bring the mind in, understanding becomes like a college education. It doesn't go deep. When our mind relaxes, we feel love and deep understanding happens automatically. It is very satisfying and it makes us happy.

Happiness thrives in a happy environment. So the best way to be happy is to make the people around you happy. You have to remember not to sacrifice yourself in order to make others happy, however. You should not feel like you are efforting to make others happy. If you are, it is the work of the ego and won't lead to real happiness. To make others happy with no interference from the ego can happen in only one way: be happy and share your happiness with others. When you are happy, you are not egoistic. No extra effort is needed to make someone happy. It happens effortlessly and it feels great.

If we have authentic love, it doesn't mean that when somebody says something negative it won't hurt us. It means that when this happens, we come to them to connect and talk. When we have love, we open the issue lovingly. It's not that we are made of steel or strong like a big wall. No, that's not love. Love is gentle, like a flower. Someone who has authentic love asks gently and lovingly. They open an issue, for example, saying, "I thought you were talking about me just now. Should we talk? I'd like to talk." This is a person with love. They have love for the other and love for themselves. That is what love is: love for all beings, including ourselves.

When we have love, we are not afraid of people. Love is very gentle, it's soft and very subtle. We don't go and fight with people. Fighting creates hate. In hate, we want to physically fight with others or put them down or be sarcastic. This is not love. With love, if someone hurts us, we understand that we just need to share with them, to talk to them gently, without defending ourselves or blaming them. Love is always gentle.

Love has immense courage. That is why we can trust when we are in love. There are three levels of love. The first level is the love of the child. It is all about taking and nothing of giving. The love of the child is the love of survival. The child needs the parents and that need gets translated into love. When you have a child's love, you are forceful and demanding. One can be a grown up and still have childish love. It is all about "me." This is the male way. In the second level of love, we want to give to others. Giving makes us feel good because we think others will like it. So this level is still about us. There is still the ego involved. The second layer is the female way of loving. The third level of love is mature love. It does not depend on giving or taking, but it embraces both. Unlike the first two layers, however, there is no selfishness in it. It is pure joy.

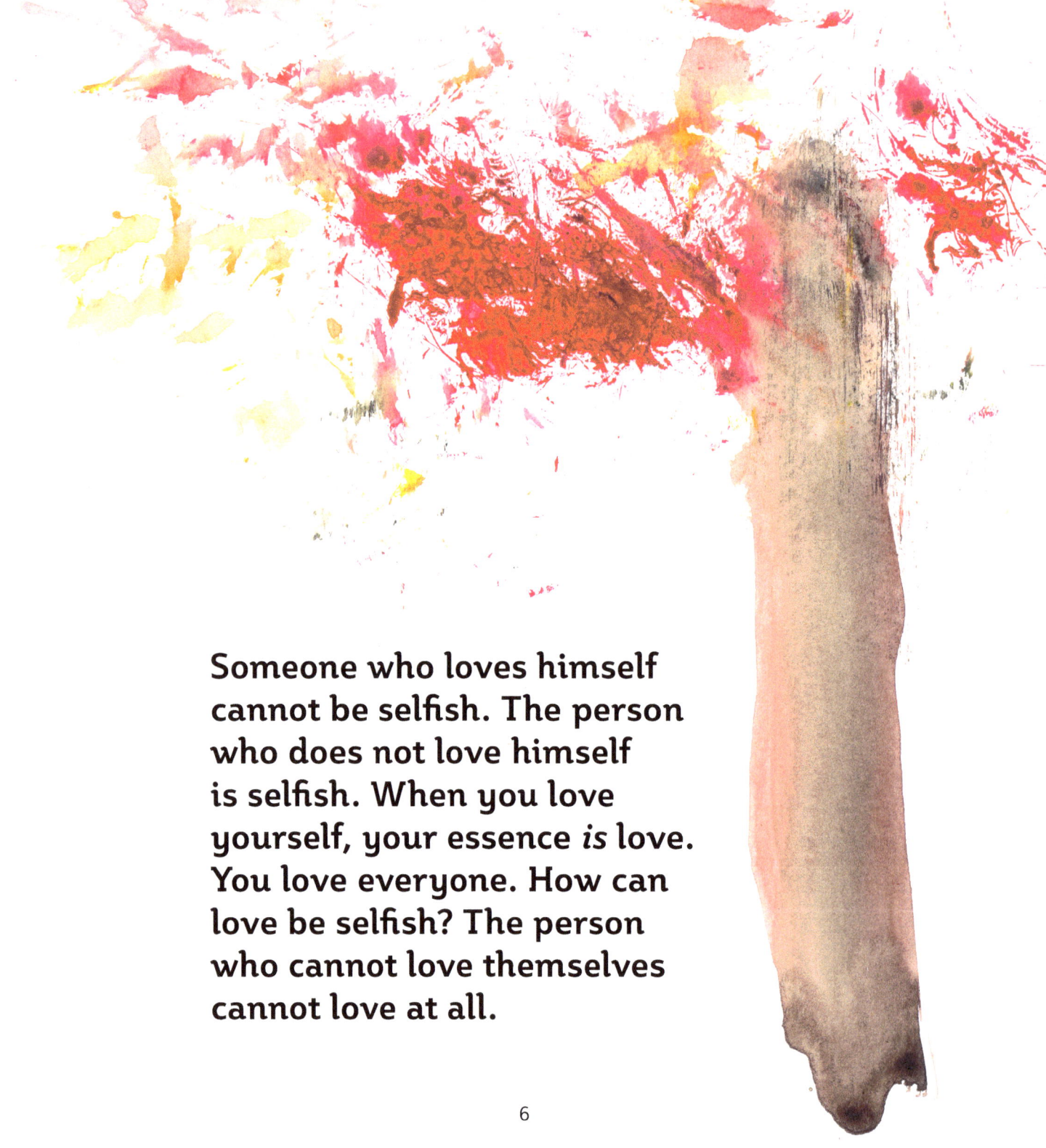

Someone who loves himself cannot be selfish. The person who does not love himself is selfish. When you love yourself, your essence *is* love. You love everyone. How can love be selfish? The person who cannot love themselves cannot love at all.

Any area where we have an emotional wound, we cannot have love. Wounds close us. Love means considering others and being open to them. So love only happens when there is no wound; when we are open. If someone has a wound in one area of their life, when that wound comes up, they close and they cannot love. But not having love in one area does not mean that person doesn't have love at all. We have to look at ourselves to see why, when we see something negative in someone, we all of a sudden can't see the positive in them anymore. This is being narrow minded. If we are open minded, we will see the whole of a person—the good and the bad together.

When the male and female energies are not in harmony, they are weak. Even their love is low quality. Female love will manifest as jealousy and male love as anger. When these two are in harmony, however, they become balanced and their love becomes compassion.

Problems like jealousy, anger, greed, and possessiveness are not really problems; they only indicate that we do not yet know what love is. All problems arise because love is not yet there. They show an absence of love. When we taste real love, we become a totally different person. We have experienced something so superior to anything else in our lives, that we literally want to kiss everyone all the time. So we cannot say I'm sometimes loving and sometimes not, prior to real love coming. We are only experiencing liking and disliking. The moment there is real love, all problems disappear. There are no complaints. It helps if we are courageous enough to see that we don't have real love, yet. So let's just be honest with ourselves; this will help our growth immensely.

Without love,
the poison in us
cannot transform
into orange juice!

Any expectation that others should love us, just shows that we do not yet have love. Our love is conditional: if you listen to me and do what I want, I will love you. When we don't have love, we expect others to have love. When we have pure love, there are no expectations. You just love, even if the other person can't. And, then, everybody loves you. You don't expect love because love is happening all the time. If we have love, love happens.

Without love,
I vanish into the
vanity of humanity.

We carry the great
in our heart
and the stupid
in our head.

When we don't have real love, we feel weak unconsciously. To counter this, we get angry to feel strong. This is also unconscious. Anger, which is male, makes us feel strong. When we have real love, a sense of well-being—a knowing that everything is okay—is there. But there are people whose heart chakras are totally closed. These people can only pretend to be nice, and only when they are forced. The power of love is very subtle and refined. It is a feeling of trusting everything and everyone. In love, we know that there is nothing to worry about. The power of love is total freedom.

What are signs that we are angry at ourselves? We eat junk food, we do not get enough sleep, we feel extremely guilty, we dislike ourselves, we think we are worthless, or we get into fights that we know will make us suffer. The list goes on and on. The ego enjoys and feels powerful when it puts people down or even when it puts us down, because it wants to feel better than. It doesn't care what kind of damage it does to our psyche or our bodies to feel this way. We try to control others, and if we do not succeed, then we start controlling ourselves. Controlling always leads to anger because something will always go against us in what we are trying to control. If we are more female, we might get sad instead of angry when our attempts to control fail. To drop this, we need understanding. Any growth needs our awareness and understanding. Becoming more aware of when we are mistreating our bodies, putting ourselves or others down, or when we are trying to control, and understanding what is behind these behaviors, helps us to expand our consciousness, which is growth.

When we are angry with ourselves, we definitely will not like others. We will find excuses to become angry at them. Most of the time, we do not even know that we are angry with ourselves. Anytime we are unhappy with life, we definitely are unhappy with ourselves. We just need to recognize this and look for the reasons why we are unhappy.

When the female gets angry at herself, she feels guilty. So, feeling guilty is the female form of anger. Men and women can both feel guilty because they both have a male and female side. It just depends on which one is stronger in the moment. And believe me, no matter who you are, sometimes the female becomes stronger and sometimes the male does. This is nature's way in every human.

You have said that we should approach problems with others gently and with love. What if, when you first open the issue, you are feeling love, but as the conversation goes on, you start to feel angry and closed?

Anger happens. It can happen at any time. You might even be angry at the beginning of your conversation. You cannot do anything about anger, it just happens. What you can do is to be on anger alert. Any time you feel angry, tell yourself right now I'm angry. I better take twenty deep breaths, in through my nose and out through my mouth, and then talk. After twenty deep breaths, the anger will go away. You have to become alert that right now I am getting angry, and I have heard Sharam say to breathe deeply twenty times and then continue your talk. Something practical!

Why is the mind negative? The mind is negative because when we are happy, the mind is mostly not there. When we are total in our happiness, when we are deeply happy, the mind stops. There is no duality. We go to our soul, and when the soul functions, we experience pure ecstasy. Nothing registers in the memory cells. When we are not total in our happiness, some memories will get stored in the mind, but it is mostly when we are unhappy, that we store negative events, thoughts, and emotions in our memory cells and the unconscious. There is no worry or anxiety in the soul. This is why we can be joyful only when we step out of our minds and into the soul.

When the mind is negative, we either get stuck in the mental body or the emotional body. In either situation, the energy has left the mind, but doesn't reach the heart. It gets stuck in one of these two bodies *because* it is negative energy. Positive energy goes all the way to the heart, where acceptance and joy live. All the positive emotions come from the heart, not the emotional body. When our energy gets stuck in the emotional body, it is gross and hurts us. We start saying things that go against what everybody else is saying. We choose antagonism and denial instead of accepting. We resist and may even go to sarcasm. Anytime you become defensive and fight, you are in the mental body. Where does the negativity in the mind come from? It depends on what we have learned as a child. It is all conditionings. All cultures have different ideas of what is positive and what is negative. We have to learn about the conditionings of our mind, so we can become aware and free.

If Existence is running the show, how is it that we are responsible for our lives?

First of all, it is important to remember that we are Existence, but because of our egos, we act like a filter. The energy of Existence passes through and manifests in us according to the cleanliness of our filter. If we have a lot of blockages or wounds clogging our filter, the energy of Existence cannot pass through us as it is. We alter it. For example, in people who are thinking heavily all the time, the energy of Existence gets stuck in their mind and doesn't flow to the chakras or the soul. In this case, it is as if the soul is absent, and the soul is the source of all joy. The mind is the source of all negativity, because all the negative memories get stored in the mind.

The content of our thoughts comes entirely from society, there is absolutely no intuition or Existence in it. So what is the mind good for? The mind is a calculator and people who are in the mind are money-minded. Money is the soul of society. Society believes the richer we are the better, but the riches that come from money are very cheap and do not create happiness.

If your filter is cleaner, which means you are more in the moment and not thinking of past memories and future desires, you will be in touch with your soul. You will be intuitive. If your filter is one hundred percent clean, you are enlightened. The more the energy of Existence can pass through you, the richer you will be, and not just with money. You will be surrounded by things like love, money, happiness, satisfaction, and contentment. You become rich in every aspect of your life.

If one is worried all the time, if there is a lot of dissatisfaction, if there is tightness with money, all it shows is that the energy of Existence cannot pass through you because your filter is not clean. In order to have a clean filter we need to trust ourselves, which requires a strong, but subtle, male and a strong female together in us. In essence, when your male and female are balanced, you operate from a higher chakra. If your male is overly strong, you become overly controlling. You want to control everything, so nothing will go wrong according to your conditionings. You will have lots of problems with people. You might be sarcastic and use sarcasm to pick on people, or you will more directly try to command people. You want to take over everything. If the female is strong and the male is weak, you are always in self-pity and guilt. You feel like a victim. If both your male and female are strong, you become more subtle. You give space to Existence to come through you, to circulate, clean up, and energize your being. You use your mind only to assert Existence's energy. The energy of love pours both into and out of you.

The best way to be your best in this moment is to stay in this moment. If you are thinking about the past or the future, for example thinking, "I should have done better," or "Why didn't I do this or that," or rehearsing what you are going to do or say next, then you are not doing your best right now. So stay in the moment and you will always be at your best.

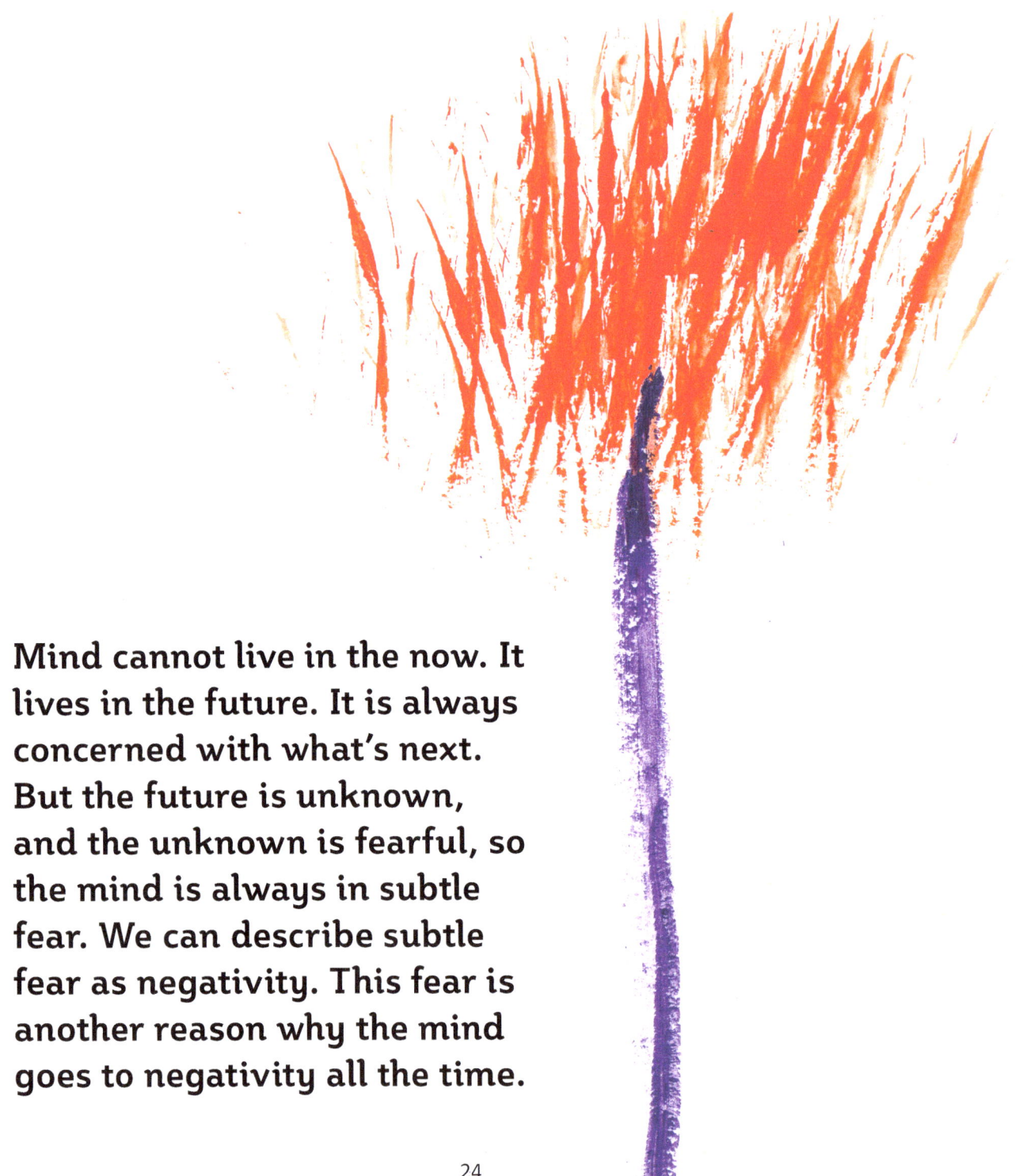

Mind cannot live in the now. It lives in the future. It is always concerned with what's next. But the future is unknown, and the unknown is fearful, so the mind is always in subtle fear. We can describe subtle fear as negativity. This fear is another reason why the mind goes to negativity all the time.

Seriousness is a disease of the mind. A serious person has a mind that goes to negativity really fast. Generally, serious people are more male; they have strong male energy. One aspect of overly strong male energy is thinking, or being heavily in the mind, and since the mind is negative it makes sense that serious people can become negative easily. A wise person is one who knows life is a play. Seriousness is a hinderance to wisdom.

Mind is the source of confusion. It brings emotional wounds into all relationships. We enter complicated relationships with our emotional wounds, and we make them even more complicated. The only way to resolve problems and make things simple is to bring the energy of the heart into situations. The energy of the heart makes everything simple and beautiful. How do we bring in the energy of the heart? We do so by paying attention to all the things we reject, because by disliking and rejecting, we go to the mind; with liking and accepting, we go to the heart.

Seeing the complexity of the mind is simplicity. You can only see how complex the mind is if you look at things with simplicity. If you look at anything more deeply, it becomes simple. Only in the mind are things complex.

**When something
is complex,
it creates problems.
When something
is simple,
it solves problems.**

People are afraid of getting their hearts broken; that is why they keep their relationships on the surface. They don't allow them to go deep. They do this because when they get hurt, their heart closes, and they don't know how to open it again. It is very hard. To protect themselves, they stay on the surface with others, not allowing a deeper love to develop. What they don't realize is that the more one's heart opens and closes, the easier opening the heart becomes until one day, the heart will open permanently. We call this enlightenment.

Why are humans afraid? Because we do not trust Existence. Fear closes us and does not let us be free. We should not be afraid of fear. We should look at it instead. Not having trust in Existence means that we have forgotten that we are one with Existence. And Existence loves us.

It loves our body and every layer of our being. Any element that separates us from others, like resisting and complaining or getting angry or emotional, makes us afraid. When there is fear, there is no trust, no love, no happiness. So it makes sense to work with our fear, to face or encounter it in order to understand it more deeply.

Trust connects you to your soul, to ecstasy.

When someone has been attacked as a child—by teachers, friends or family—as they grow older, they become afraid of people. They tend to stay in the background, hide, resist or disagree with others all the time. Their fear has developed in the form of passivity or aggression. Then because they are afraid, they cannot love. They are so occupied with fear, they have no room for love. When their fear steps aside, with the help of understanding, love arises.

There are two kinds of passivity. One passivity resists and the other passively receives. Most people, when they are passive, resist. But being a passive receiver is very beautiful. It is basically accepting.

The ego can appear in different forms—some egos are aggressive, some are passive. All egos want to destroy other people's egos, but ego destroys others at the price of destroying us. The passive ego hurts others through resistance. It pushes people away with resistance. It has a subtle tone of blaming others. The passive ego has learned that resisting bothers others, so it resists to punish them. But this resisting hurts the person that is resisting *and* everyone around him. It separates him from others. If we see the games of our ego, we have the power to stop it. The reason the ego wins is because we don't see its subtle games. It operates from our unconscious. If we become aware of and accept the ego, it steps aside by itself.

Ego is just a mentality. It is an illusion and not a good illusion either. It is more like a nightmare, because our ego likes it when we suffer. Suffering makes the ego feel more important. It is proud of its suffering and misery. Happiness isn't acceptable in society. It makes you look irresponsible. But if you suffer, people love it. Suffering makes the ego happy and society approves. Because of this mentality, people try to hide their happiness and are proud of their suffering. In the world, you cannot be important or valuable if you are happy. But if you are suffering, you are very important. This is another reason why we focus so much on problems. The ego creates problems out of just about everything, so we can suffer and share our suffering with others. Seeing this game of our ego will eventually make us free of it.

Ego is basically what we call an inferiority complex. Everyone, somewhere in their life, has been told they are not good enough by parents, friends or society. So to one extent or another, everyone has an inferiority complex. This is why the ego is always trying to prove that it is great. One way it does this is to create problems, so it can solve them and feel better. If the ego cannot create problems for itself, it finds other people's problems and tries to solve them to feel better. This is why we make our lives such a great struggle, because the more problems we solve, the better we feel about ourselves.

We (our egos) need to be liked by others or we feel tense and unhappy. The reason for this happened when we were very young. Our parents felt obligated to teach and train us for our own well-being, according to what society said was right. Every time we did something that went against society's values, they yelled at us or showed their dissatisfaction. But as babies and children, we had very gentle souls, so all this was very harsh for us. And it's not our parents' fault, they were treated the same way by their parents and so on down the line. But now, every time someone doesn't like or approve of us, we go back to that memory of intense harshness, and we become unhappy. If we deeply understand that we are not our past, we can be criticized and stay in the here and now. Others can say something negative about us and we are able to hear it. We understand that all humans have both negativity and positivity; the negative is as much part of us as the positive and just as necessary.

The "I," or the ego, is empty; it has no substance and is constantly worried others are going to find this out. It tries very hard to protect itself, to make sure nobody finds out how empty it truly is. If I think someone has discovered I am worthless, I am going to fight, feel bad or get hurt, which only shows that I feel worthless inside. If I felt worthwhile, I wouldn't put out the type of energy that makes people want to criticize me in the first place. Other people sense our feelings of worthlessness and respond accordingly. We all have the "I," so we take things personally. We look for the tiniest thing to fall apart over and feel bad about. We have to look at this and be aware of it when it is happening.

If we like someone for any reason, it definitely comes from the deeper part of us. When we dislike someone, it comes from our surface— the ego. When we like them, it is Existence inside of us liking that person. The ego is the source of all disliking.

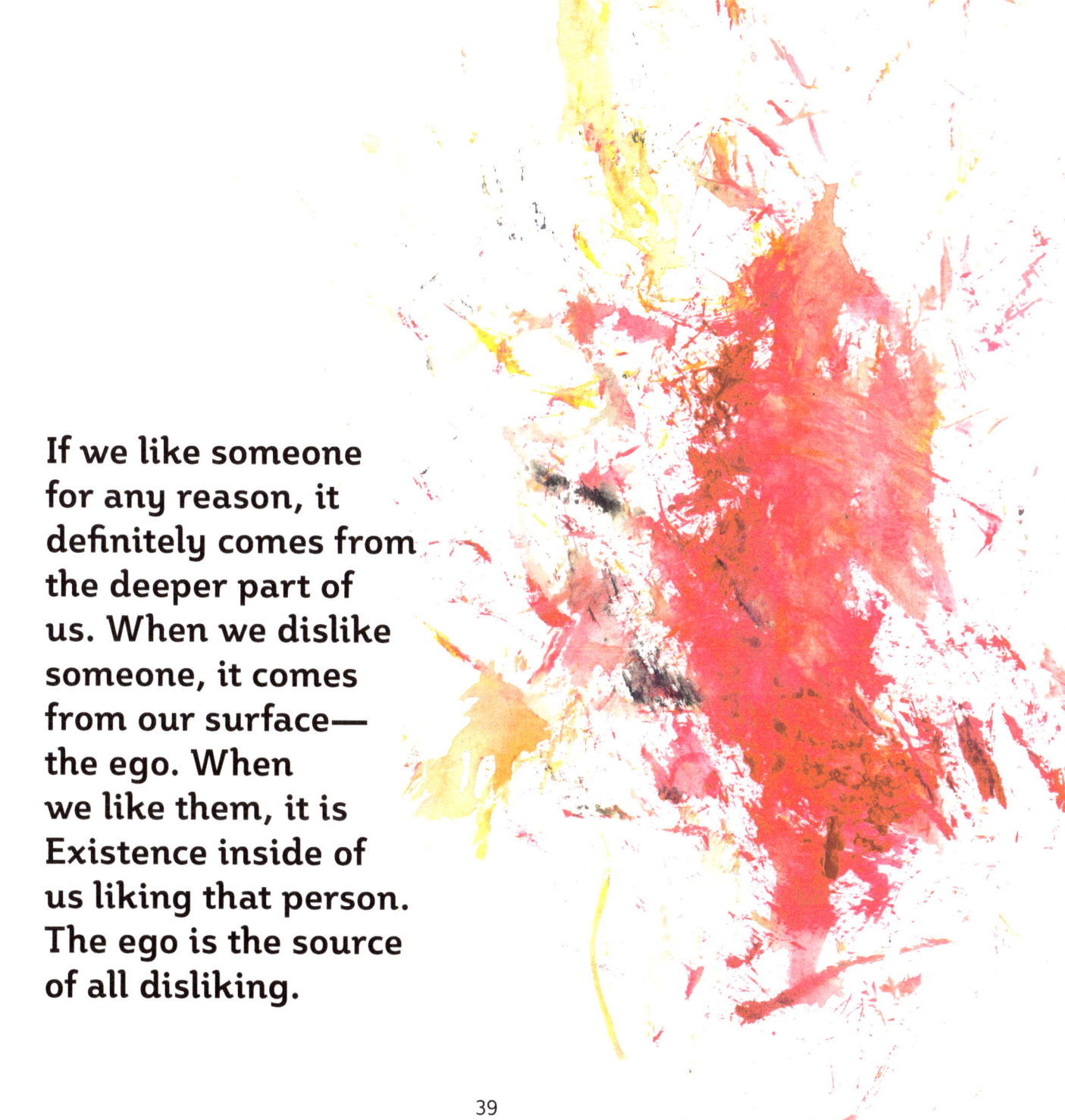

Sometimes we create illness to get attention and sympathy from others. But we know that if we stay sick for too long, they will start taking our sickness for granted, so we make sure we get better. Then, after a while, we come up with another sickness. It is good to see the games of our ego.

Everyone comes to a point in life where things become really hard. This is our opportunity to look at our ego and face it. Unfortunately, most the time, we don't have the courage to face ourselves, so we lose this opportunity. The ego is afraid of being exposed; it does not allow us to be courageous. But that is the only way out of its trap.

We need subtlety to see the ego and courage to expose the ego. We need to be subtle and brave. Seeing the ego and exposing it is the only way to destroy it.

It shouldn't be discouraging to have an ego. We should recognize that having an ego is necessary for us to get to know ourselves and to grow. The ego reveals all of the things that keep us from experiencing our souls: things like our conditionings, wounds, negative memories, hate, and jealousies. I have heard people say, "Hey, I have an ego, what do you expect? I can't stop my anger or not be demanding. Egos don't have love. It's impossible." And then they don't look at themselves. They don't want to work on themselves. We shouldn't use the ego as an excuse to support our negativity. That is not love. Love is, "Okay I do have an ego, but that doesn't mean that I cannot have love. I will work toward that," instead of, "I have an ego, it's impossible."

On the inner path, the ego is just a stepping stone. Ego is the ugly side of humanity. The ugly side is there to make the beautiful side stand out even more. It highlights the beautiful. This planet, being dual, causes everyone two have to sides, the ugly and the beautiful. Our job is to transcend this duality. When we do, we enter the Divine.

When we don't like something and fall apart, we are working against the will of Existence. But even that is fine because we are still a part of the Existence. Existence happens through us in both lower and higher qualities. When we resist and get hurt, we are operating out of the lower qualities of Existence. But this is good because this hurt motivates us to work on ourselves to go to our higher chakras. It is through the higher chakras that the higher qualities of Existence gain access to us. In the higher chakras we don't resist, so we don't get hurt. We have a choice whether to go with the lower or the higher, but we don't know we have a choice. That is why we often operate from the lower levels without wanting to be there. Our life becomes one of high quality when we are in the higher chakras. In the higher chakras, we don't get bothered as much. If someone else is in a lower chakra, we can see it, but it doesn't affect us. We give space to others and don't get entangled with them. We see life as the play of Existence. Getting entangled with others is part of the lower chakras.

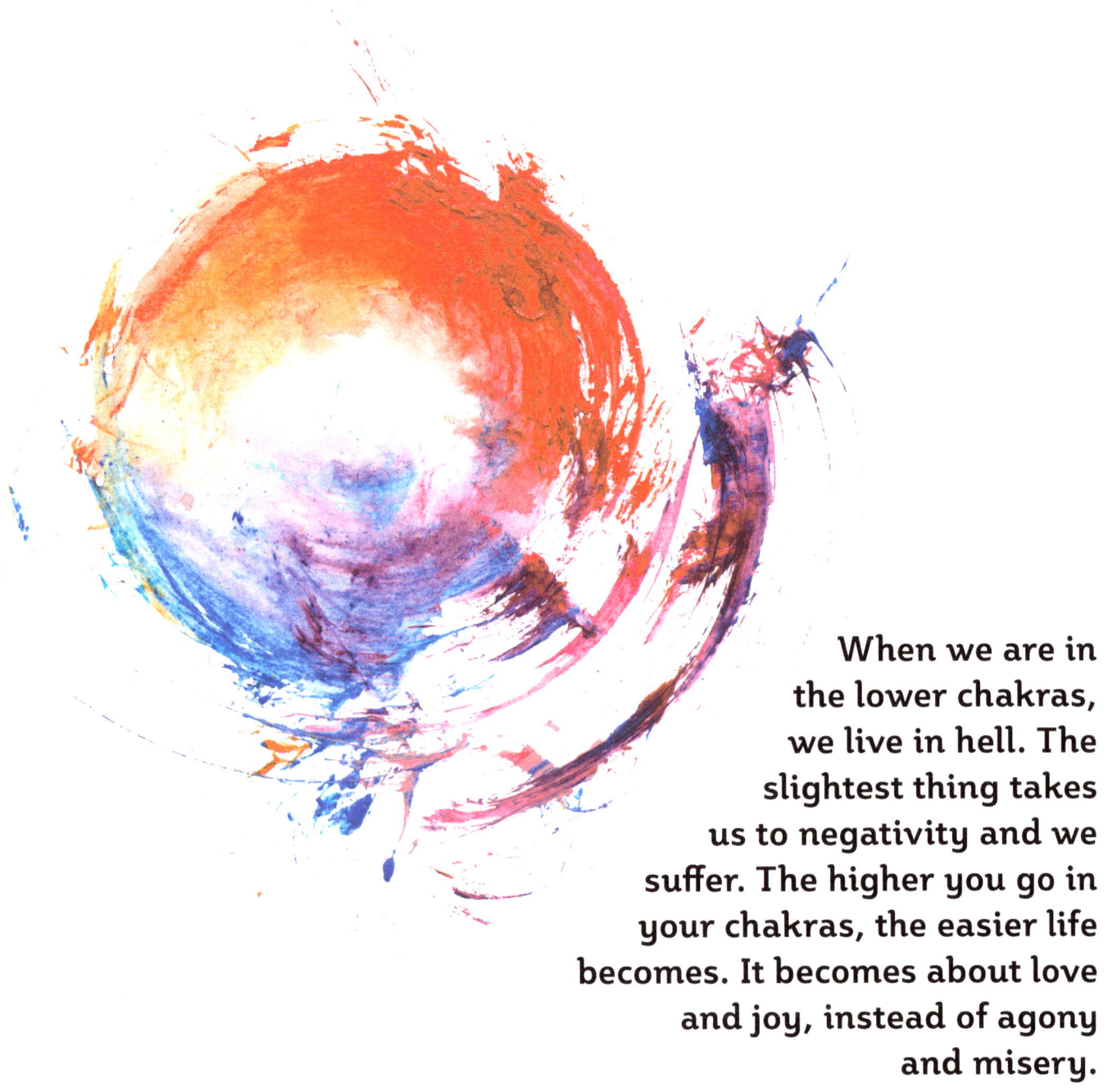

When we are in the lower chakras, we live in hell. The slightest thing takes us to negativity and we suffer. The higher you go in your chakras, the easier life becomes. It becomes about love and joy, instead of agony and misery.

Every time we transform, it means that we bring the light of the higher chakras to the lower chakras. We bring subtlety, beauty, and gentleness from the higher chakras to the lower. Then the lower chakras open up. This opening is transformation. It is basically cleansing the lower chakras of karma and bringing light to them.

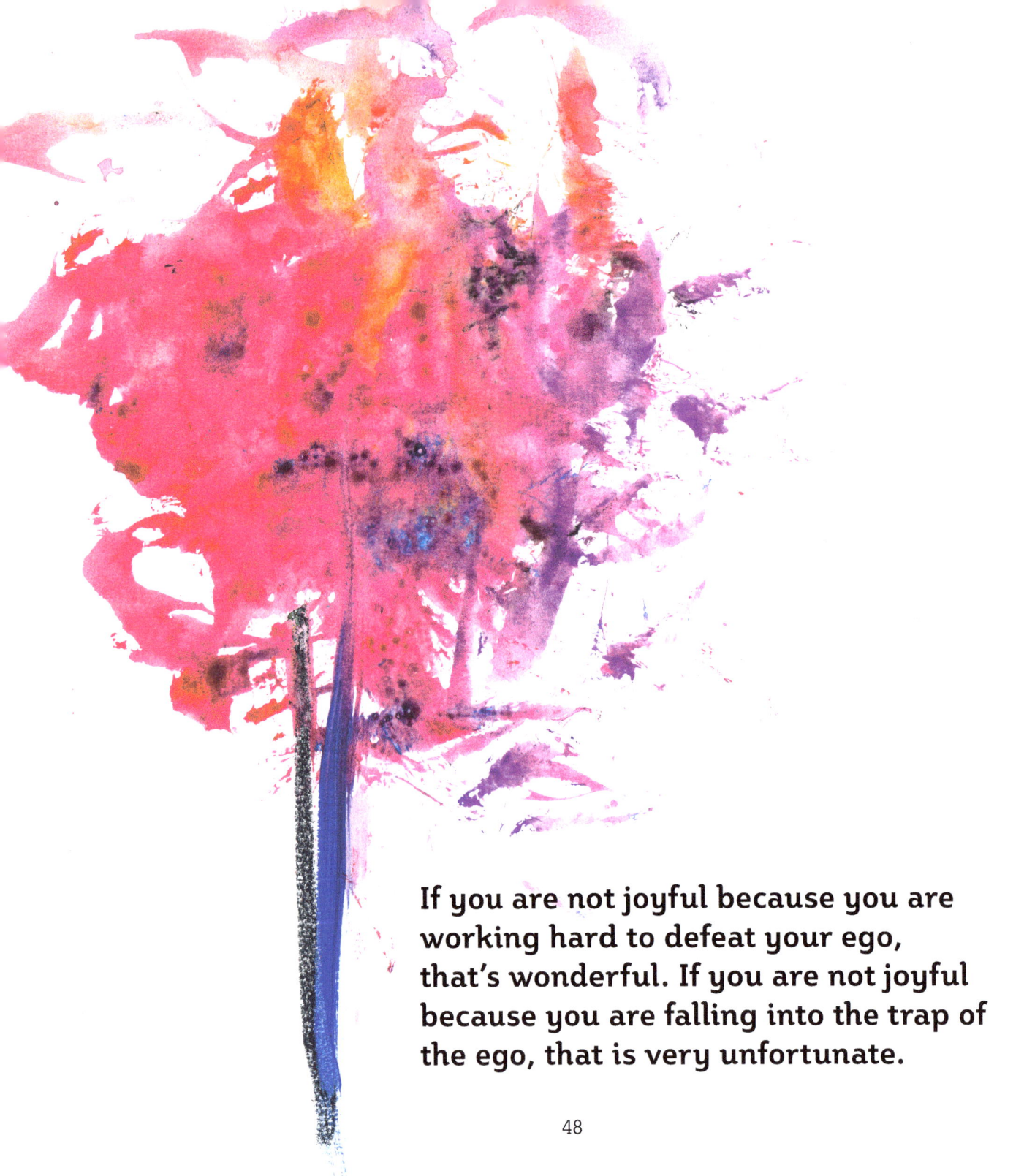

If you are not joyful because you are working hard to defeat your ego, that's wonderful. If you are not joyful because you are falling into the trap of the ego, that is very unfortunate.

Emotions and thoughts are part of the ego. Emotions are a major part of the female ego, and thoughts are a major part of a male ego. Someone who has more male energy goes to the mind and mostly stays there because that is the definition of male: to be in the mind. Usually, a person with more female energy doesn't go to the mind much. The essence of nature is female, and there is no mind in nature. When someone is very female, they are on the same level as nature, so they too do not go to the mind. When something negative happens, they may go to the mind at first to come up with strategies to protect themselves, but because they can't stay there, they fall into the emotional body, which is all emotions.

The "I" is incapable of doing anything. So if "you" want to change something in yourself, it is basically impossible. The "I" is the ego, and it cannot destroy itself. The only way to change something in us is to bring awareness to the problem. With awareness the energy of our soul enters our physical, emotional, and mental bodies and heals our wounds. We are still doing it, but indirectly. We are doing it by stepping out of the "I".

Existence is always in harmony. Only humans fall from harmony. Why? Because our egos want to create a world of their own—separate from others. Hence, man becomes an island and loses contact with all other parts of Existence, with the total. Mysticism is a bridge that takes man from the island back to the mainland. The ego is destroying you. It is destroying your harmony and your joy. So cooperate in any way you can with destroying the ego.

There are three levels of awareness. In the first level, awareness is low. People in this level don't take responsibility for themselves, their actions or feelings. They are totally irresponsible. They blame everyone for everything and have a victim mentality. In the second level, awareness is growing more and more. This group of people takes responsibility on themselves. As their awareness grows, they blame and complain less and less. In the third level, awareness is fully developed. This person understands that the ultimate and only responsibility is to trust Existence, to trust that everything that happens is necessary and absolutely the love of Existence for all involved. When we understand this, there is absolutely no reason for blame or complaint.

We should not meddle with or bother trying to change our personality, emotions or behaviors. This meddling is just an attempt to make ourselves a little bit better, but the very effort of trying to change ourselves is futile. We need to know that as long as we are in this body, our personality will stay with us. It will stay with us, but that does not mean that it is us. It is more like the shirt you are wearing right now. You can put it on and take it off whenever you want. How? With awareness and acceptance. With awareness, we come to know our personality with all its positives and negatives. But to become aware, we also need to accept that it is there—especially the parts we don't like. The more total our acceptance, the easier it is to see our personality. With awareness and acceptance, we distance ourselves from our personality and all its problems. We step out of our personality's influence on us. And when we step out, everything seems so unimportant. We get to see how primitive and childish our personality is. We see that it has been passed down to us from our ancestors and has no relevance anymore. Life becomes a play when we look at it from a distance. It is only when we lose our distance, that we get entangled with life and feel frustrated all the time.

In order to grow,
we don't need to
change our patterns;
we need to recognize
and see them. By seeing
them, they change automatically.
We start acting from a higher quality,
and suddenly, we notice that our
patterns have changed. Recognizing
or seeing with awareness is magical.
It brings the energy of our soul into
the different patterns of our lives.

All of our lives, we have been taught to take things seriously. Now, on the path of inner, we hear over and over that we should not be serious, that playfulness is a basic quality of a spiritual person. Why? Because if we are always serious, we become mentally, emotionally, psychologically and physically unhealthy.

Understanding, acceptance, love, and laughter are all elements that can take us out of our seriousness. Although laughter is amazingly healing, deep inside we feel guilty when we laugh because there is always a voice in our head that says, "People are suffering. You shouldn't be irresponsible and happy." We might not know it consciously, but subconsciously, everyone feels guilty when they laugh. Being loving, on the other hand, is something that has been praised all our life, so we feel very good about it. Since being loving takes us out of our seriousness and, deep inside, we have acceptance for it, it is one of the best ways to get out of seriousness.

We have to understand one thing though, and that is we do not have to change ourselves. Our essence will always be the same. If we are a serious person, we will remain serious no matter how much we grow, but the quality of our seriousness will change. We will become total in our seriousness, which will bring a higher quality to everything we do. The fact is, in worldly matters, if we are not serious the work we do will not be high quality. Playfulness does not mean we do not take our affairs seriously, it's more that we are playfully serious. When we are playfully serious, we understand that we are above the things we do, we are divine. We can stand away from it all. With this let-go, we are more creative in our doings and our interactions with others. We are curious and open, while still getting the job done. This freedom and let go is playfulness.

Awareness means becoming more aware of our own being. The more aware we become, the more familiar we are with our being. In this way, the mind becomes more silent. Awareness is recognizing the silence of our soul. When there is calmness, all of a sudden understanding happens. We call this an inner jump. We feel and understand our soul in that moment.

We are here to transform through *self*-realization, or realizing and recognizing ourselves; but instead we keep trying to analyze and realize others! Let's focus on ourselves. It is the only way out of darkness, misery and deadness.

Whenever you doubt, you give power to negativity. When you doubt, you make the negative possible. Even when we doubt someone else, our doubt makes them do the negative things that we doubted them for in the first place. Then we blame them for doing these negative things. If we look deeper, then we see there is no room for blaming. Doubt is okay, because all negativity is there to help us grow, but when we blame others, we refuse to grow.

People who are perfectionists always doubt. They doubt because they are afraid things might go wrong, but the reality is, sometimes things go wrong. Perfectionists have experienced this in the past, so they are afraid, and doubt themselves and others, and their abilities. The more doubt you have, the less confidence you have.

We are political or we cover up our real selves because we do not trust our ability to deal with situations as they come up. We want to prevent certain situations from happening, so we learn to become controlling and political. The person who trusts his ability to deal with things is totally free and in let-go. He is open and kind, and if problems arise, he responds in the moment. Part of the reason why we do not think we are able to deal with situations is that we condemn emotions and natural instincts that are rejected by society. We don't allow our emotions or others' to be expressed. Instead, we become unclear and controlling in order to avoid feelings we have been conditioned to believe are uncomfortable or unacceptable.

When we defend ourselves, divine energy does not come in, so we become depleted of energy. Divine energy comes in when we are open and ready to receive.

Ego happens when we get entangled with our or others' issues. Ego means getting entangled with conditionings, memories, old wounds, karmas, negative thoughts, and emotions. All of this usually leads to blaming others.

When we are balanced and stay centered, we can go into an issue with a person who is blaming us, and work through it. Our centeredness helps not only us to see our role in the problem, but it helps the one who is blaming us to acknowledge their part in it, too. Basically, blame disappears.

When our awareness is small, we easily get affected by the thoughts and ideas around us. As our awareness grows, these thoughts and ideas affect us less and less because of our own deeper understanding. Whatever we do, we do it according to our awareness and understanding.

If someone is acting awkward and we feel awkward around them, that just shows how unaware we are. We fall into others' energy instead of having our own center. And it's not just awkwardness, this applies to all kinds of emotions like anger, sadness, hate....

Having a person in your life who is a goof-off helps you to become wise. You have no choice but to take responsibility.

When someone tries to make us feel guilty, if we are mature, we won't fall into their game. But if we do fall into it, we just need to remember that this is an opportunity for us to become mature and stay centered.

Maturity comes with seeing
the subtleties in ourselves and others.
The more we can see the subtleties,
the more mature we are.

People have a conscious mind and an unconscious mind. We are aware of our conscious mind and therefore have control of it, but we are not aware of our unconscious mind, so it operates outside of our control. A woman's conscious mind comes from her mother and her unconscious mind comes from her father. It happens more often than not that if our mother is tough and harsh, our father is passive and nice. A daughter from this couple, then, would get her conscious mind from her mother. So her mother's harshness will be in her conscious mind, but since we have control over anything in our conscious mind, this woman would have control over her harshness. She will be nice to the people she loves, but can also be really harsh to people she doesn't like. A boy in this same family would get his conscious mind from his father and his unconscious mind from his mother, so deep inside the boy will be harsh and tough, but because it is in his unconscious, he will have no control over it. This person won't be very nice. The opposite also applies. If the father is tough or angry, the daughter becomes angry and the son will be in control of his hardness. Knowing all this helps us to look at our patterns and conditionings and become aware of who we are.

The more we understand, the smaller our emotional baggage. With understanding, our unconscious mind transforms to the conscious. Becoming emotional is an unconscious phenomenon. So when we are more conscious, we become less emotional and less worried.

**Awareness and acceptance
heal our old wounds.**

Awareness does two things for us. First, when we are aware, we don't make karma. For example, when you enter a room with awareness, you don't judge people. You don't think negative thoughts about others. The second thing awareness does for us is to protect us from getting karma from others. When we are aware, we don't get negative energy from others when we are with them.

When we are unhappy, there is only one reason for it—we are disliking something. Liking and disliking are manmade. They come from the mind and our culture's beliefs about good and bad. These beliefs have been imposed on us. If we become aware, we can see these patterns and become free of them.

Creativity in understanding or meditation will make us enlightened.

We want people to respect us, but for this to happen, we must first respect ourselves. If we value ourselves, other people will follow suit. If we do not value ourselves, others won't either. People treat us the way we treat ourselves. Our ultimate value comes from understanding and the inner freedom that comes with understanding.

One understanding can change a narrow mind into an open mind.

When we are emotionally hurt, any logic we or others use to ease the hurt won't help. The only thing that helps is an understanding. Logic is the opposite of emotions. In order to get out of emotions, going to the opposite is not going to work. Going beyond opposites is the only way out and that is understanding.

The only way the male and female can unite is with understanding. This male and female could be an outer male and female or our inner male and female. Because we are born from a mother and a father, we have part of each of them within us. We have the male part on the left side of our brain and the female part on the right side of our brain.

Mind doubts; it dislikes and has problems with everything. We cannot drop the negativity of the mind because the mind and negativity are the same thing. The only way to get out of negativity is to get out of the mind and into the heart. Many times, we'll have negative thoughts about someone that we would like to express to them, but we don't. We try to hide our feelings. We do this because there is a subtle judgment about expressing negative thoughts that makes us feel guilty. But the truth is, when we express ourselves, we become free of our negative thoughts, and then we can like the person again. It is good that we express, but it is not always good to express our feelings to the person we feel negative about. Sometimes, it is best to hide our feelings from them because we do not want to infect them with our negativity. All it would achieve is to close their heart.

    But we still need to get this negativity off our chests, so we talk to someone else about our feelings. We see, then, that talking behind others' backs is very freeing for both ourselves and the person we are taking about. Existence is all love. Cultures make us feel guilty about so many things. They make us feel guilty about expressing our negative thoughts about others to them and, at the same time, they tell us we shouldn't talk behind their backs. Also, we hate it if we think someone is talking behind our back. But, now, we see how healing it is; we are getting rid of our negativity without closing another's heart. When we bring understanding to a situation, we act out of awareness and not the conditionings of our cultures.

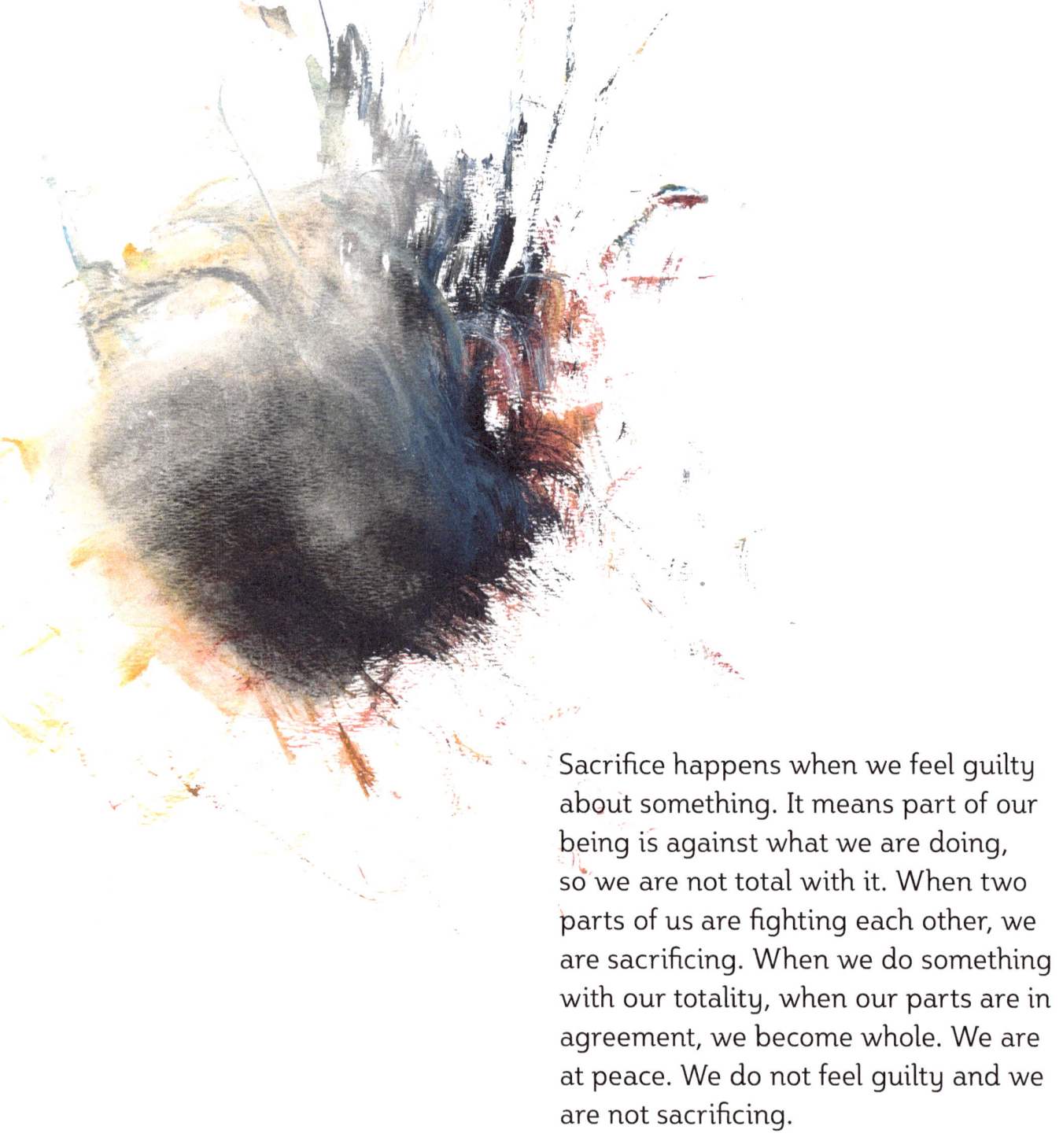

Sacrifice happens when we feel guilty about something. It means part of our being is against what we are doing, so we are not total with it. When two parts of us are fighting each other, we are sacrificing. When we do something with our totality, when our parts are in agreement, we become whole. We are at peace. We do not feel guilty and we are not sacrificing.

If we think people see us as unintelligent, we get upset. We get upset because deep inside we think we are not intelligent. We don't have self-confidence. Deep inside everyone feels less than. We think we are not good enough. We also criticize others for not being good enough, so we can feel better than them.

    The way to gain self-confidence is through deep understanding. We are here on Earth to understand and become confident. Earth is a place for souls to gain faith in themselves and Existence. We live in a world of better or worse, a world of dualities. Deep understanding helps us to drop all dualities.

Inferiority and superiority exist only in our minds. In Existence, there is no inferiority or superiority. Expectation comes from inferiority; and demand comes from superiority. In general, female energy expects and male energy demands. But remember, a man can be more female and a woman can be more male. So regardless of your sex, if you are more female in any moment, you will have expectations, and if you are more male, you will be demanding. Only with deep understanding do we go beyond superiority and inferiority, beyond male and female to the land of God.

When we take advantage of others, we lose self-confidence. Confidence is basically one's inner power. Having inner power brings us whatever we need in life, including satisfaction. So, by taking advantage of others, we lose not only our confidence and inner power, but also our satisfaction in life.

Judgement comes from feeling inferior. When we are a perfectionist, we always feel that we are not good enough, and we hate ourselves. So we judge others and put them down to feel better. Or we brag. Bragging is another form of putting others down. So feeling inferior is the root of self-hate and judgement.

If we go through life
trying to be useful all the
time, we will go mad. Usefulness
and uselessness should be balanced in life.
If everything is done only because it is useful,
life becomes dull, imbalanced and miserable.
Uselessness brings relaxation and enjoyment to life.

Everyone is a perfectionist to one extent or another. When we are a perfectionist, we want to be perfect so others will like us. One way to be perfect is to prove other people wrong. At the same time, it is very hard for the perfectionist to accept any criticism, or to acknowledge that they have been wrong. So, we see how hard it is for the perfectionist to grow.

Perfectionism and the path of love often go together. People on the path of love just want to be loved. But our conditionings and the dual love/hate nature of most all relationships has taught us that we have to be perfect to be lovable. If our path is love, then, we don't want to hear any criticism, because, that means we are not perfect. If we are not perfect, we believe we are not lovable; and we have to be lovable to be loved. So we fight tooth and nail to be perfect. If somebody, God forbid, says something negative about us, we don't want to hear it because we immediately think we are not lovable. We defend and resist in our effort to be perfect, but defending and resisting themselves are not lovable. They only manage to separate us more from the ones we love.

The only reason things go wrong is because we do not trust ourselves. When we do not have trust in ourselves, chances are that whatever we do will go wrong. We are very powerful beings; whatever we believe, happens. If we believe we can do something, then we can do it. When we doubt ourselves, we are unsure if we can do something, so there's a fifty/fifty chance of failing. Whatever happens is entirely up to us. Our soul decides everything.

The only reason we compare
is because we are not
sure of ourselves.
If we are sure of ourselves,
we do not need to compare.

When we do not expect, we appreciate, and with appreciation there will be no complaints. Appreciation takes us to our soul and the soul is pure ecstasy. Expectation takes us to the mind and the mind is pure negativity. Comparison is a subtle form of expectation.

When we compare, again we are not appreciating. Why? Because the moment we compare, we go entirely to the mind; we are not satisfied with how things are. Comparison pulls us down from the ecstasy of the soul to the heaviness of the mind. Fairness is one of the many ways we have been taught by society to compare. But fairness often isn't really fair, because our minds don't want to believe that we have any flaws. Our fairness is one-sided fairness. Let me tell you a story.

When Mr. Smith received his paycheck at the end of the month, he noticed that the company had paid him two hundred dollars too much. He went home happily without telling anyone. The next month, when he received his paycheck, he noticed it was two hundred dollars short. He immediately went to the accountant and complained.

The accountant replied, "But last month, you received two hundred dollars over what you should have. Why didn't you complain then?"

Mr. Smith replied, "One mistake is okay, but two in a row, I just can't go for."

This is what we call one-sided fairness. When the mind compares it goes to judgment with an unfair perspective. There is always the "I" over others. Expectation by its very nature is unfair. Expectation means wanting people to do things to please me regardless of who they are and what they want. Unfair expectation causes separation among people and friendships to fail. It makes us and/or others miserable. Appreciation, on the other hand, always brings us to love.

When we are creative, we don't get bored. Boredom comes from having expectations and desires. The less expectation and desire we have, the more creative and content we become.

We are a drop in the ocean. When we worry, we are separated from the ocean. When we are not worried, we become one with the ocean. Worrying comes from fear. Fear that is not so condensed becomes worry and anxiety. Condensed fear is terror.

Judgment means pushing someone away and separating the self. When we judge, we become a drop separated from the ocean. We do it because the ego feels better than others when it judges. Ego is that subtle thing in us that wants to be better than others all the time. If it acts harshly, it is easier for us to see, but mostly it is very subtle and hard to catch.

One body has billions of cells and each cell has a specific role. When all the cells unite and work together, they become part of a much bigger body that can do amazing things. Like the body, humans are all cells in a body we can call God, the Beyond, or Existence. We can separate ourselves from the Beyond, but when we do, we become small and we suffer; or we can be one with this limitless and beautiful body. In oneness, we contain all the planets, galaxies, suns and moons. Another way to look at it is the drop and the ocean. Each person is a drop in a vast ocean that includes all of Existence, but the mind or the ego insists on separating. Instead of being the ocean, the ego wants to be a drop. It thinks it makes it unique, important and special, when all it really does is make us miserable. The truth is there are no drops in the ocean, there is only the ocean. There is no separation. It is just an illusion of the mind. This is the only thing we have come to Earth to learn, nothing else.

When we have a problem with anyone, it is our problem, not theirs! By telling people the problems we have with them, we are throwing our responsibility on them. Existence wants the person to be like that. Who are we to object? Actually, they are Existence and by not liking them, we are not liking Existence. We could almost say, we are the enemy of Existence when we do not like someone. Our ego might say, "But others do the same thing." So what? If others want to hurt themselves, that doesn't mean we have to do the same.

When understanding comes, Existence takes away anything we don't need anymore. For example, we don't need worrying or anxiety. This is why, when we start to understand, we become relaxed and happy; sadness goes away.

When we are in the mind,
everything is divided into
positive and negative.
When we go beyond the
mind, everything is one.
There is no duality.
We feel unity.

Existence has three layers: the negative, the positive and the Beyond. The Beyond is the layer of our soul. It is beyond the duality of positivity and negativity. We drop into the negative whenever we experience the slightest thing we do not like. For example, we are cold or late or hungry…. The negative layer of Existence is very sticky; when you go there, it is very hard to get out. Unlike the negative layer, it is very easy to fall out of the positive. If we perceive any tiny thing as negative, we fall. The Beyond is even more subtle. We only reach the Beyond when the mind is quiet. All it takes is a single passing thought for the Beyond to disappear. One thought and we are back in the duality of positivity and negativity. As we mature and gain more subtlety, we can stay in the positive, or the blissfulness of our soul longer.

When love flows, negativity goes.

When we breathe mostly from the left nostril, we become more female; our male is reduced. When this happens, we feel insecure, and the slightest negativity turns into a huge catastrophe. So we see that the left nostril converts our breath into female energy, and the right nostril converts our breath into male energy. This is incredible. If both nostrils are evenly open, then we become centered and don't fall apart as much.

The energy of the etheric body, the body that connects our physical body to our spiritual bodies, becomes strong when our inner male and female are in harmony with each other. This harmony or balance allows energy to be saved in the etheric body instead of getting wasted in the mind. When you are in harmony, you choose when to use the mind and when to set it aside. Energy goes to the mind only for as long as we want. But because male energy has dominated our culture for so long, our male and female are not balanced. Our energy goes to the mind all the time; we waste our energy thinking. We do this because when we aren't balanced, we feel weak and want to become strong. Basically, thinking is male. People also associate strength with the male, so by thinking, we are increasing our male energy in an attempt to become stronger. But we get stuck in the male, thinking all the time, and then we can never become balanced.

When we sit and don't do anything, energy starts moving into the etheric body, helping us to feel stronger. The more energy we store, the stronger we feel. When the etheric body is strong, we no longer need to think to feel strong. With thinking, we suffer because of all the negative memories stored in the mind. The smallest thing reminds us of something negative stored in the mind and we suffer. But...this suffering is necessary. When we suffer and get ourselves out of it into non-suffering, and we repeat this again and again, we make our soul stronger. Therefore, even suffering is for our growth. So remember when you are suffering there is always a good reason for it. This doesn't mean I am promoting suffering, but if it is happening, we might as well look at the positive side of it.

If we feel worthless inside, we put out an energy to others that says, "I don't matter." Then no one cares about us. People are part of Existence, and they reflect our energy back to us. This is one law of Existence, and it actually shows Existence's love for us. When people reflect our negativity back to us, we go through hardship and eventually have to learn from it and grow. Before we really understand this, we might get mad at others when we think they are not taking us seriously, but that is only because we can't see that we put out that negative energy first.

On the inner path, our enemy is our friend, because they point out our negativities. Since we are on a mystical path, hopefully we will be open to hearing about our negativities and use what we've heard to work on transforming them. With transformation, we become lighter and freer. What could be better than that?

Humans have three layers, the surface (the unreal), the real, and love. In the first layer, we pretend everything is fine; we sugarcoat everything and hide our negativity. The second layer, which is deeper, is where we keep all the hate and problems we hide from ourselves and others when we are in the first layer. In the first layer, we know what we hate about others, but we try not to go there. The third layer is pure love. In this layer, we love everyone and everything. It is the deepest part of us. People rarely get to this layer, though, because to get there, we have to pass through the second layer, which scares us. So everyone stays on the surface; they never get to real love. We can get through the second layer by acknowledging our negativity, expressing it, and not being afraid.

Repression happens when negative energy gets stuck in our soul. This negative energy carries a specific kind of information. For example, it may contain a memory about a situation or person who hurt us or made us feel powerless, or something that scared us or made us angry. It could be any kind of negative information. We call this information an emotional wound, and once it gets stuck in our soul, we continue to act from the information stored there until we recognize and clear it.

People who fall apart often, do so because as children, they were not given space to express themselves and convince others to do what they wanted. They had to fall apart, cry, or get upset to get what they wanted. This becomes a deep habit and stays with them. Even as adults, they become upset and fall apart if the slightest thing goes against their will. Paying attention to this will help these people to not fall into this pattern as easily.

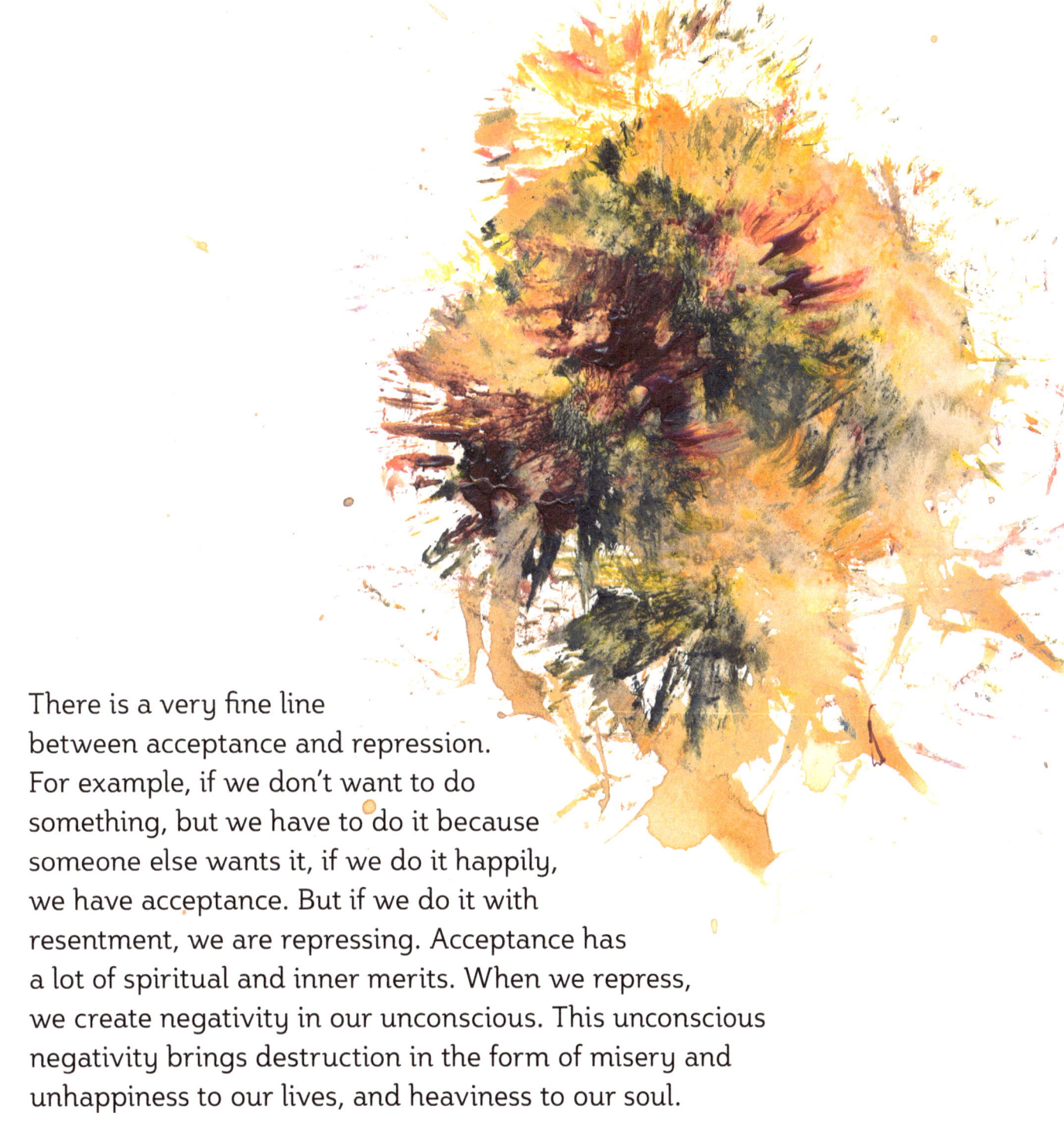

There is a very fine line
between acceptance and repression.
For example, if we don't want to do
something, but we have to do it because
someone else wants it, if we do it happily,
we have acceptance. But if we do it with
resentment, we are repressing. Acceptance has
a lot of spiritual and inner merits. When we repress,
we create negativity in our unconscious. This unconscious
negativity brings destruction in the form of misery and
unhappiness to our lives, and heaviness to our soul.

Any state we go through is beautiful. Anger, sadness, fear—they are all beautiful. Why? Because, if we accept them, they give us immense insight into our life. They give us the opportunity to grow and experience happiness. We always have the choice to accept and go to happiness or reject and go to unhappiness.

Nothing is ever wrong. We are all growing, meaning we all have areas of our life that need to improve. This is the nature of life. Knowing this, we can live a relaxed life.

Human beings are dual—for example, we are both good and bad. We have both, but we reject the negative, or the bad. We are here on Earth to look at the negative, to understand and accept it. When we do this, we move beyond duality. Because it is impossible to not have duality and be alive on Earth, if you are alive, you have both good and bad in you. Negativity helps us grow. It is absolutely necessary for our growth. If everything was always good, what motivation would we have to grow. In fact, if everything was good, we would stop growing and our lives would stagnate. There would be no joy or aliveness.

Earth is the planet for growth. If you had already done your growing, you wouldn't be here. So as long as we are here on Earth, we need to have the bad to grow. If we hate to hear about our negativity, then we are in trouble. Criticism is essential to our growth. It is pointing to a negative part of us that, if we learn about and transform, will act like the rung of a ladder for us to step on and go higher. The biggest criticism we can say about anyone, then, is that they are "uncriticizable." Basically, it means the person doesn't want to grow.

The biggest problem people have is to think they shouldn't have any problems. Problems are there to help us grow. The only way out of a problem is to acknowledge it, to own it. If we own our problems, we become free of them. The reason people get stuck in their issues is they reject they have them, and instead, project them onto others. They stay focused on others, so they cannot see themselves.

We carry one main issue with us from one life to another. This may seem frustrating, because we think it means we are not getting anywhere on our spiritual path, but it is in fact a blessing. We carry our problems in the unconscious, so if we had many different problems, our unconscious would become so huge, it would be impossible to overcome. Having one main problem keeps things simple. Even if we don't believe in past lifetimes, it works for this lifetime as well. Fewer problems repeated over and over simplify life. With each encounter of the same problem, we gain more understanding. Society expects us to solve problems quickly and be done with them, but that is just a lack of deeper understanding.

The only reason we are here on earth is to learn how to accept all negativity. When we accept everything, Existence rewards us with enlightenment.

In order to have a strong etheric body, we need to connect with Existence. When our center becomes one with the center of Existence, the energy of God pours into us. When this happens, you never lack energy. But how do we connect with the energy of Existence? We connect through acceptance. In any moment, if you accept, you become full of energy. If you resist, you lose energy. Your etheric body becomes weak and you become depressed. Also, you can easily get sick. When you accept, you get plugged into the of energy from Existence, directly. Then if a sad or angry person comes near you, they won't affect you. They might take your energy, but you are so full of energy, you won't even notice. When you accept, you end the separation between you and Existence. You become one with Existence. When you reject or resist, you separate from the whole and your battery becomes weak. Then any small thing will disturb you and cause you to fall apart. When you accept, you get more energy and when you get more energy, it is easier to accept. In general, any falling apart, any temper tantrum, any disturbance, any passive resistance means the energy of the etheric body has become low from not accepting.

Acceptance happens when we are in the moment. If we carry the past with us, we will find it difficult to accept. The more we experience the moment, the more it becomes a part of us, and the easier it gets to let go of the past.

Spirituality means
to accept whatever is.
When we accept
whatever is,
we become spiritual.
If we don't accept,
we leave spirituality.

Paintings by Sharam
View and purchase giclée prints

Visit:
SharamLove.com

www.ingramcontent.com/pod-product-compliance
Lightning Source LLC
Chambersburg PA
CBHW041550220426
43666CB00002B/25